# VOICES

## AFRICAN AMERICAN AND HISPANIC STUDENTS' PERCEPTIONS REGARDING THE ACADEMIC ACHIEVEMENT GAP

DuPage County Regional Office of Education

### Dr. Darlene Ruscitti
Regional Superintendent of Schools

Written by:

Lourdes Ferrer, Ed.D. & Stephen Garlington, MSW/LCSW

Title: **Voices**

Subtitle: **African American and Hispanic Students' Perceptions Regarding the Academic Achievement Gap.**

Authors: Lourdes Ferrer, Ed. D & Stephen Garlington, MSW/LCSW

Description: This book is called *Voices* because it captures what African American and Hispanic students believe deters them from reaching the full measure of the American Dream. *Voices* simply echoes the thoughts and feelings of the students of DuPage County.

Printed in the United States of America

Published by:

DuPage County Regional Office of Education
Dr. Darlene Ruscitti
Regional Superintendent of Schools
http://www.dupage.k12.il.us/

ISBN-13: 978-1477415238     ISBN-10: 1477415238

# DEDICATION

We dedicate this book to the many committed DuPage County educators who work tirelessly to provide students with the best education possible.

.

# VOICES

# FORWARD

This book is called *Voices* because it captures what African American and Hispanic students believe deters them from reaching the full measure of the American Dream. *Voices* simply echoes the thoughts and feelings of the students of DuPage County.

The stated mission of the DuPage Regional Office of Education is to collaboratively build and sustain a high-quality county educational community for all. Dr. Darlene Ruscitti, DuPage County Regional Superintendent of Schools, is determined to see this mission lived out to its fullest. In keeping with this intent, she determined that the academic achievement gaps evidenced by African American and Hispanic students must be addressed.

Dr. Ruscitti, with the financial support of the DuPage County Board, hired Lourdes Ferrer, Ed.D. and Stephen Garlington, MSW/LCSW to address the needs of under-achieving minority students. As part of their work, they conducted hundreds of interviews with high-achieving minority students over a five-year period to ascertain the students' perspectives on the academic achievement gaps. High achievers are more able to articulate orally and in writing their perceptions and yet close enough to their peers to provide insights about students who struggle academically. Out of the analysis of the students' responses, 25 significant findings emerged. In response to these findings, Dr. Ferrer and Mr. Garlington propose a series of 27 actionable recommendations, which are offered in this book. The implications for the education and political communities are boundless.

Educators are held accountable for the performance of all students. With today's focus on test scores, schools cannot continue to allow significant performance gaps to exist. This book outlines specific problems and provides clearly delineated solutions. This work goes beyond the theories to offer concrete ideas that can make a significant difference in the academic attainment of these deserving students who so obviously need assistance to achieve their full potential.

African Americans and Hispanics represent approximately 30% of the population in the United States and their numbers are increasing. Their educational attainment and contributions to society will significantly impact the future of our nation. It is a moral and national imperative to address these gaps for the betterment of these students and our nation.

In the words of Dr. Ruscitti, "As educators, we have a moral imperative to educate all our children well. It is the foundation of our democracy, our economy and the American Dream. We can do it! We have the expertise, the political will and the greatness of heart."

# CONTENTS

# PROLOGUE

# PROLOGUE

## How the Meaning of a Quality Education Evolved

In the Agricultural and Industrial eras, determination and a strong work ethic were sufficient to open the doors to a quality life in the United States. Times have changed. In the current Information era, these two character traits, though important, are not enough. It is a quality education that provides the gateway to a quality life. The meaning of the American Dream has also changed over the course of history. In the past, it meant the availability of low-cost land for farm ownership. In today's era, the American Dream is the opportunity for one's children to receive a quality education and career without social or economic barriers.

The definition of a quality education is not static. It will continue to change based on the knowledge and skills students will need to earn a decent living at a given place and time. Our schools' current academic curriculums are far more rigorous than those from decades ago. Students are now required to master academic content at earlier grade levels and they must do so at "microwave" rather than "conventional oven" speed. Also, a high school diploma alone no longer prepares students for our current job market. Eighty percent of the fastest growing job categories in the United States require a post-secondary education. To be employable and ensure that our nation remains competitive in our knowledge-based, highly-technological and global society, more students must reach higher levels of education than previously experienced in the history of our nation.

A quality education demands that students reach proficiency in two very important core subject areas - reading and mathematics. Why reading and mathematics? Students who are competent readers are better able to become independent life-long learners - a vital skill in our continually evolving society. Additionally, students who are competent in mathematics internalize critical-thinking and problem-solving skills - abilities that are needed to resolve the challenges of our times.

President Obama, in his 2010 State of the Union address noted, "The rules have changed. In a single generation, revolutions in technology have transformed the way we live, work and do business. Sustaining the American Dream has never been about standing pat. It has required each generation to sacrifice, struggle, and meet the demands of a new era." In keeping with the spirit of his message, we believe that students' proficiency in reading and mathematics is a pre-requisite for meeting the educational demands of our current era.

In 2001, under President George W. Bush, the No Child Left Behind (NCLB) Act set expectations for all children to demonstrate proficiency in reading and mathematics as determined by each state's annual accountability test. The purpose of this law is to ensure that all children have equitable opportunities to obtain a high-quality education. Further, this law holds schools accountable for all students' educational proficiencies in both reading and mathematics irrespective of race, ethnicity, socio-economic status, level of language acquisition, learning disability or immigration status. NCLB contains the most sweeping changes to the Elementary and Secondary Education Act (ESEA) since its implementation in 1965. NCLB is based on two major intrinsic values of American society - every child can learn and no child should be left behind.

## When the Gaps Emerged

As all states began reporting their annual accountability test results by subgroups, performance gaps began to emerge. Limited English Proficiency (LEP) students and Students with Disabilities (SWD) are the subgroups with the lowest percentages of students who score at proficiency levels in both reading and mathematics. Students belonging to the Black, Economically Disadvantaged and Hispanic subgroups follow respectively. White and Asian subgroups have the highest percentages of students who score at proficiency levels.

These test performance gaps begin in the third grade, the first year that the NCLB law mandates that states test students. Unfortunately, these performance gaps are sustained through the last year of testing in high school. Having a learning disability or lacking mastery of the English language can, in large part, explain the lack of achievement for these two subgroups. It is more difficult to justify the performance gaps that persistently exist between African American and Hispanic students compared to their White and Asian peers.

According to the 2011 Illinois State Report Card, 85% of White and 89% of Asian third grade students demonstrated reading proficiency on the 2011 Illinois Standards Achievement Test (ISAT) compared to only 61% of Hispanics and 61% of African Americans. During that same year, 64% of White and 66% of Asian eleventh graders demonstrated reading proficiency on the Prairie State Achievement Examination (PSAE) compared to 33% of Hispanics and 25% of African Americans. Similar gaps were also observed in the mathematics portions of both tests. This disappointing phenomenon is replicated in most, if not all, of the accountability tests results reported by other states.

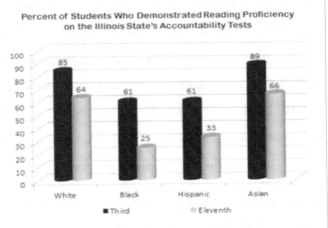

Percent of Students Who Demonstrated Reading Proficiency on the Illinois State's Accountability Tests

Educational leaders are aware that performance gaps have existed between African American and Hispanic students and their White peers since the inception of standardized testing. The National

Assessment of Educational Progress (NAEP) has reported these gaps since the 1970s.

Disparities regarding academic success are manifested in other areas as well. The Pew Hispanic Center reported that, according to the 2008 American Community Survey (ACS), 18% of African Americans and 37% of Hispanics age 20 or older did not hold a high school diploma or General Education Diploma (GED) compared to only 10% of Whites and 14% of Asians. The same source reported that only 50% of African Americans and 36% of Hispanics had some post-secondary education compared to 61% of Whites and 70% of Asians. As previously stated, today's knowledge-based, highly-technological and global society requires all students, regardless of race or ethnicity, to acquire levels of education beyond high school.

This lack of academic achievement has a profoundly negative impact on the employability of African American and Hispanic students. According to 2010 U.S. Census data, these two ethnic groups represent 28.9% of the population in the United States. Therefore, due to the size of these two populations, their lack of academic achievement will have a wide-reaching adverse impact on our country by weakening the nation's competiveness in world markets.

## What Research Says

There is an extensive body of research that exists in this area. When analyzed as a whole, current research indicates that there are several predominant reasons for the achievement gaps that exist between African American and Hispanic students and their White and Asian peers. Three of those reasons are:

1. Students from these two ethnic groups are more likely to be instructed by under-qualified teachers, or qualified teachers that lack preparation to teach traditional academic content to students who are not proficient in the English language or lack expected grade-level knowledge.

2. Students from these two minority groups often attend schools where learning environments are not conducive to academic success. In these environments teachers have low academic expectations, instruction is poor and students are alienated. These schools usually have safety problems and the rates of detentions, suspension and expulsion are typically high.

3. African American and Hispanic students are frequently exposed to ineffective teaching practices. That is, instruction that is delivered at the same time to the whole class and which emphasizes lecture, drill and practice, student seatwork, etc.

To help more African American and Hispanic students achieve greater academic success and to reduce the achievement gaps that exist between them and their White and Asian peers, we must acquire a better understanding of the students in these two ethnic groups.

## What it Means to be African American or Hispanic

African Americans and Hispanics are usually referred to as "minorities" or "people of color", which implies sameness between the groups. However, these two groups have different histories, cultures, and challenges.

## Hispanic

In the United States, Hispanic is a term used to identify a wide range of nationalities and races that have Spanish as their primary language. We must understand that this ethnic group is profoundly diverse not only in race, country of birth, nationality, and citizenship, but also in primary language skills, prior educational experiences, and socioeconomic and immigration status.

For example, Carlos is a Hispanic student whose parents are from the Dominican Republic. Carlos was born in the United States and therefore, is a U.S. citizen. His race is Black. His education has taken place entirely in the United States and he prefers to communicate in English though he is fluent in Spanish.

Carmen was born in Guatemala and immigrated to this country illegally. She considers herself a "mestiza" (Spaniard/Indigenous). She received most of her education in Guatemala and prefers to communicate in Spanish.

While Carlos and Carmen are considered Hispanic because they both share Spanish as their native or maternal language, they differ in their language of preference, country of origin, race, and residential status – Carlos is a born citizen and Carmen is undocumented.

According to the 2010 Census, Hispanics now comprise 16.3% of the U. S. population, making them the largest minority group in this country. The United States currently has the second largest Spanish-speaking community in the world, second only to Mexico.

Culturally, Hispanics are generally characterized as people who deeply value family. The family is perceived by Hispanics as the transmitter of their culture and the vehicle for achieving individual goals. Hispanics are known for having a very strong work ethic. Most Hispanics immigrate to the United States determined to work hard to improve the quality of their lives. They also rely heavily on their faith to assist them to overcome challenges and realize their aspirations.

## African American

In the United States, African American or Black is a term used to identify people who are citizens or residents of the United States with origins in any of the Black racial groups of Africa. The term is generally used for Americans with sub-Saharan African ancestry. Most African Americans are the descendants of captive Africans who survived slavery and segregation within the boundaries of our nation. However, there are also those who are descendants of immigrants from Africa, the Caribbean, South America and other parts of the world.

For example, Joseph is an African American student born and raised in the United States whose parents and previous generations were also raised in this country. He speaks only English.

Abebe is considered African American because he is Black even though he was born and raised in Ghana. Abebe came to this country legally. He is fluent in English but prefers to speak Akan, one of Ghana's recognized dialects.

While Joseph and Abebe are considered African American because they both share the same racial classification, they differ in their language of preference, country of origin, and residential status in this country – Abebe is a legal resident and Joseph is a born citizen.

According to the 2010 Census, African Americans or Blacks now constitute 12.6% of the U.S. population making them the second largest minority group in the country.

Culturally, African Americans can be characterized as people who embrace family and fictive (non-blood related) kinships. Within their family structure, mother figures are held in particularly high regard. African Americans are likely to embrace fictive kinships to obtain and receive support. They are prone to have a heightened sensitivity towards injustice because of their historical struggles against slavery and segregation, as well as contemporary adverse micro-messages regarding African Americans. Blacks also tend to find refuge in their faith and derive strength through community worship.

Both African Americans and Hispanics have made great contributions to the America we know today. Through the media we are made aware of significant contributions in the arts, sports and entertainment industries. Less apparent are the important roles that these two ethnic groups have played in our government, military forces, economic development, educational systems, and scientific advancements. And, although African Americans and Hispanics have their own distinctive cultures, important components of these cultures have been woven into the fabric of our nation.

# What Forces Deter Academic Achievement

To further enhance the understanding of African Americans and Hispanics, it is important to explore the forces that continue to deter many of these students from achieving greater academic success. The two forces we believe to have the most significant and wide-spread negative impact are the Hispanic "family divide" and the African American "cultural split."

## The Family Divide

In her book *Hispanic Parental Involvement: Ten Competencies Schools Need to Teach Hispanic Parents*, Dr. Ferrer coined the term "family divide" to describe a chasm which forms between Hispanic parents and their children caused by linguistic, cultural, technological, educational, and immigration-status gaps. These five gaps lead to a divide that breaks down the family structure the same way that cracks in a foundation can cause a house to fall.

Dr. Ferrer asserts that language, cultural, technological, and educational gaps occur when school-aged children of Hispanic families enroll in the American educational system and ascend through higher grade levels. Hispanic children move up the ladder of language acquisition (from "silent to proficient") and acculturation (from "honeymoon to adaptation"). These students also achieve mastery over technological innovations and often achieve higher levels of education than their parents. While these progressions are occurring, their parents' English language proficiencies, stages of acculturation, technological skills and educational levels frequently remain stagnant. Immigration status gaps occur when children are born in the United States, making them citizens though their parents do not have legal status.

It is Dr. Ferrer's belief that the linguistic, cultural, technological and educational gaps can adversely affect communication between the parents and children, creating generational misalignments of values, beliefs, attitudes and perceptions. These gaps can also lead to role-reversal situations in which parents become dependent upon their children. These gaps can also impede parents from becoming active participants in their children's education. The immigration-status gap can create significant anxiety regarding the possible deportation of one or both parents leading to a family's emotional, social and financial crisis. Parents who are undocumented are likely to avoid communicating with teachers and will avoid participating in school events due to the fear of being "outed." This furthers a sense of isolation and deepens the divide between parents and children.

The family divide gaps constitute forces that threaten the Hispanic students' abilities to achieve expected academic proficiencies. They represent barriers that must be acknowledged and addressed in order to close the academic achievement gaps that exist between Hispanic students and their White and Asian peers.

## The Cultural Split

When looking for underlying reasons to explain the achievement gaps that exist between African American students and their White and Asian peers, we subscribe to the concept of an African American cultural split. According to Mr. Garlington, the author of the essay *It's a Matter of Choice*, the "cultural split" is a term that can be used to describe a generational ideological rift that divides the African American community into two camps: those who continue to rationalize that racism and discrimination will trump any effort to pursue the American Dream, versus those who embrace acculturation and view education as the legitimate process for upward mobility.

Mr. Garlington asserts that African Americans who believe that racism and discrimination will trump any effort to succeed see the world through a "victim-ology" lens. They operate from a victim mentality. This group of African Americans does not feel that they are part of mainstream American culture. Students who are socialized in this manner appear to have the lowest levels of academic achievement and may subscribe to the premise, "It ain't gonna make no difference." These students are more likely to enroll in lower track courses and exhibit behaviors that are not conducive to academic success and may express outward resentment towards their same-race peers who embrace education.

On the other hand, African Americans who embrace acculturation and education as the gateway to a quality life are more likely to see the world through a "victor-ology" lens. They operate from victor mentality. These African Americans see themselves and their children as bona-fide citizens in today's America. Despite some of the still present vestiges of racial injustice and inequality, these African Americans believe that determination and a strong work ethic can result in overcoming these barriers. In other words, they subscribe to the premise, "Yes, we can!" Students who are socialized in this way appear to have higher levels of academic achievement. These students are more likely to enroll in rigorous academic courses and strive to achieve a higher grade point average. Unfortunately, the students who seek academic success and speak Standard English as opposed to street vernacular or Ebonics are often ostracized by their same-race peers.

The victim-ology lens of the cultural split is a force that threatens the capability of many African American students to reach their academic potential. Therefore, this negative mental frame-of-reference must be acknowledged and addressed in order to close the academic achievement gaps that exist between African American students and their White and Asian peers.

## What Came Next

We have learned much about achievement gaps exploring existing research and analyzing students' performance on regional, state and national standardized tests. We have also drawn on the professional knowledge, experience, and wisdom of the DuPage County Regional Office of Education (ROE) consultants and the DuPage County school districts' superintendents, principals and teachers.

Despite these rich knowledge resources, we felt it was important to go a step further – to reach out to and learn from African American and Hispanic students themselves. After all, it is the students who attend our schools, decide which courses to take and earn the grades. It is the students, and not the experts, whose futures are at risk. We focused our efforts on high school students because the performance gaps are more pronounced at this level.

Since 2006, under the leadership of Dr. Darlene Ruscitti, DuPage County Regional Superintendent of Schools, numerous studies have been conducted to ascertain students' perspectives on the reasons behind the stubborn performance gaps reflected on the ISAT and PSAE. Due to the nature of the research, a qualitative versus a quantitative approach was utilized. Although quantitative studies are known to be more objective and the data collection is more efficient, qualitative studies can provide an in-depth understanding of the factors which play a significant role in the students' attitudes and actions regarding their education.

In accordance with qualitative studies best practices, school-site focus groups and individual interviews took place with hundreds of African American and Hispanic high school students from across DuPage County. Vast quantities of valuable and insightful student responses regarding the academic achievement gaps were accumulated.

Fifty percent of the students who participated in these studies were African American and 50% were Hispanic. All were at the highest levels of academic and behavioral standing compared to their same-race/ethnic peers. These students were more likely to have the skills to articulate their thoughts and feelings both verbally and in writing. But they were also close enough to their same race/ethnic peers to provide insights about students who struggle academically or demonstrate behaviors that are not conducive to academic success. The students who participated did so voluntarily and with parental consent.

During the interview processes, students participated in an interactive PowerPoint presentation. They were then prompted to respond, first as a group and later individually, to the following questions:

1. Why are African American and Hispanic students' performances on the reading and mathematics portions of the PSAE lower than their White and Asian peers?

2. What do you think the school could do to help more African American and Hispanic students improve their performance in school and on the PSAE?

To increase the students' comfort levels while sharing their ideas, the African American students met with Mr. Garlington and the Hispanic students met with Dr. Ferrer. The students' verbal responses to these questions were captured using digital recorders. Later, each student responded in writing via computer to the same questions. The facilitators captured their written responses on flash drives. Great care was taken to preserve the integrity of the students' verbal and written responses and to honor their confidentiality. The students' responses were later analyzed in search of emerging themes.

## What We Learned and What We Did

The DuPage ROE's academic community continues to be positively impacted by the findings that emerged from these studies. We were delighted by the students' desire and willingness to share their thoughts and ideas. The students stated that they felt validated by the process and motivated to pursue greater academic success.

While many of the study findings confirmed what the DuPage ROE academic community already knew, other findings were profoundly revealing. For example, it was apparent that African American and Hispanic students' perceptions regarding their peers' lack of academic achievement were, in many cases, distinctly different. It also became clear that many of the reasons for their peers' low academic performance were associated with home and community circumstances rather than school. Students attributed many of their same-race/ethnic student academic failures to personal and cultural factors. Although some of their ideas regarding what schools could do to help them improve confirmed many of the initiatives already in place, others fueled our desire to adapt new approaches to help these students improve academically.

As a result of these studies, a higher level of awareness was obtained regarding the personal, family, cultural, community and school circumstances that adversely impacted the African American and Hispanic students' academic achievement. This new level of awareness prompted Dr. Ruscitti to develop the ROE Equity and Excellence Department. This department has launched many initiatives which include: Illinois State Board of Education (ISBE)-approved academies for school administrators; workshops about diversity and cultural competency for school staff; consulting and technical assistance for school districts regarding African American and Hispanic students' issues; school and county motivational workshops for African American and Hispanic students; *Navigating the American Educational System* (NEAS) parent involvement workshops in both English and Spanish; and partnerships with educational and civic organizations.

Dr. Ruscitti believed that what was learned from the DuPage County students was important to share with the rest of the academic community. She felt it would be of particular benefit to those who are committed to helping more African American and Hispanic students achieve their full potential and close the stubborn performance gaps reflected on the states' accountability tests. Therefore, she commissioned the writing of this book.

# FINDINGS

# FINDINGS

## Emerging Findings: What Students Think

Of the following 25 findings that emerged from the studies, 12% (3) were derived from the African American students' responses, 32% (8) from the Hispanic students' responses, and 56% (14) from both ethnic groups.

Each finding was evaluated as Low, Medium or High, based on the number of times the theme emerged in the students' responses. Only 4% (1) of the findings were identified as Low, 20% (5) were identified as Medium, and 76% (19) were identified as High. Each of the findings is followed by some of the students' quotes that support the finding. The students' quotes have been slightly edited to improve clarity.

# FINDING # 1

## Students have a negative attitude towards the Prairie State Achievement Examination (PSAE).

*African American and Hispanic Students/Level of Intensity: HIGH*

Both African American and Hispanic students consistently expressed negative opinions regarding the PSAE. According to the students, their performance on the PSAE has no impact on their high school academic careers. The PSAE results do not affect their Grade Point Average (GPA) and doing well on the test is not a graduation requirement. They believe that the true purpose of the PSAE is to evaluate their schools' performances and not their individual academic abilities. Some students stated that the ACT portion of the PSAE, which is administered on the first day, is viewed as practice for later taking the examination when it has real consequences. There were students who said that the PSAE was not a fair measure of their abilities. The manner in which it is formatted and administered does not allow students to demonstrate their true reading and mathematical skills. Most students also stated that the test was simply too long. It is difficult for students to stay motivated and focused for such a long period of time over two consecutive days.

*"The PSAE does not affect my GPA and I will graduate no matter what, even if I just bubble in anything and fail. So, why bother?"*

*"I believe that the students are not trying their hardest when they take the PSAE. I know I did not try my best either. The PSAE is just a test that the state of Illinois uses to gather some statistics."*

*"I try my best on the ACT part, the first day. That way I know how the test is and that way I am more prepare to take it again. For me it is like a practice."*

*"Students do not try their hardest because they know the test results do not give the most accurate results of their abilities. Kids who excel in math and reading may not do so well on the PSAE because of the way the questions are asked. I think some kids never do well on standardized tests."*

*"The test is just too long. Many students are burned out and mentally worn down; so, they cannot recover to take the PSAE at their full potential."*

# FINDING # 2

## Students lack the knowledge and skills to succeed academically.

*African American and Hispanic Students/Level of Intensity: HIGH*

Both African American and Hispanic students regularly stated that they lack the knowledge and skills needed to do well in school and on the PSAE. They lack the reading comprehension and mathematics skills to enroll in courses such as chemistry, physics, pre-calculus, etc., which could better prepare them for post-secondary education. They also stated that the content measured on any standardized test was higher than what they were learning in class. Their reading and mathematics abilities were not at the level necessary to answer the test items correctly and within the allotted item time frame.

*"It is very hard for me to do my homework because I have a hard time understanding what the books say. The teacher wants us to read the whole chapter and then answer the questions at the end of the chapter. It takes me a long time because I read too slow and have to read the same thing again and again until I get*

it. *I never liked to read. I read like a middle school kid, below grade level. At least, that's what my reading teacher says. I take a reading class now."*

*"I took the PSAE last year. I am a senior now. That test was too hard, at least for me. There were many math questions about stuff I never saw before. What I am learning in high school does not match the test. I was supposed to answer questions a lot faster than what I am used to, like in less than a minute or so. In school, teachers give you more time to read things and answer the questions."*

*"I feel that if we gave our full effort, we could be equal, if not higher than any other races. I'm an African-American and my classes include pre-calculus, Spanish, physics and other classes like that. The hard classes really prepare you for college. But, I will admit that in all of my classes about one other African American is in that class. And, sometimes I'm the only one. Where are the others? They are just as smart as me but they do not put forth the effort. They only take the easy classes."*

# FINDING # 3

## Students are not proficient in the English language.

*Hispanic Students/Level of Intensity:* **HIGH**

Hispanic students strongly believed that a lack of English proficiency prevented current and former ELL students from achieving higher levels of academic success. Students who lack English proficiency have little or no access to a rigorous academic program and little hope of doing well on any standardized test. The lack of English proficiency also reinforces the tendency of ELL students to remain isolated from the mainstream student culture and to refrain from participation in extra-curricular activities. Students stated that the inability to effectively communicate in English contributes to a profound sense of hopelessness.

*"Some Hispanic students don't know a lot of English. They might sound like they do but in reality they don't. They still have problems understanding everything they hear in class or read, and might not be able to write as good as the other kids in*

*class. I am not in Bilingual anymore, but I still feel that I don't know as much as the other students do."*

*"We have to learn English from scratch. Hispanic students try to speak English and learn it so they don't stay at the bottom. Sometimes, we are embarrassed of speaking in English in class because we don't know the language to perfection. So, I don't raise my hand when the teachers ask questions."*

*"There are a lot of clubs in school that I would like to join. But, I am afraid because they (students) all speak English so well. I still speak with an accent, a little bit. I am afraid they will make fun of me."*

*"I don't think it is right what they do with the bilingual kids in this school. They keep us separated from the rest of the school. Most of our classes are in Spanish. How are you going to learn English that way? We are not learning fast enough. What hope do I have for a career?"*

# FINDING # 4

## Students do not value a quality education.

*African American and Hispanic Students/Level: HIGH*

A significant number of African American and Hispanic students believed that too many of their same-race/ethnic peers simply do not see the value of education. They have not internalized the connection that exists between their performance in school and their future quality of life. Earning a high GPA or doing well the PSAE are not graduation requirements. They do the bare minimum to earn their diploma.

*"My theory is that the African Americans want to play all day and never do work. Overall, African Americans have their priorities mixed up. Males want to go to the NBA (National Basketball Association) without doing any (school) work. But, it's not easy anymore. You must have a good education. The African American male also wants just to get by and hope for some type of miracle of some sort. I think that they think just coming to school and hopefully graduating is good enough. I know that just coming to school and passing the classes with mediocre grades are not enough."*

*"Many Hispanics think that taking hard classes like honors or AP is not important. For them, graduating high school is good enough. All they want is to pass the classes, no matter the grade. I think this is because many Hispanic parents never graduated. When I say to them, 'Listen, you are not getting a good education!' They say to me that they just want to graduate and then work. Many Hispanics come to the United States just to work. Not me. I want a good education."*

*Overall, Africans Americans and Hispanics really don't value education because they watch too much TV, BET (Black Entertainment Television) or all the African American and Hispanic celebrities, instead of looking at reality. It's okay to pattern yourself as a celebrity or an NBA player. Just make sure that you have a good education so you can make it in this world. I think that not doing well in school or a test like the PSAE can have a great effect on the African American and Hispanic societies."*

# FINDING # 5

## Students do not take personal responsibility for their own academic achievement.

*African American/Level of Intensity: MEDIUM*

Some African American students believed that their same-race peers tend to abdicate responsibility regarding their own academic performance. They appear to externalize blame for their lack of academic achievement. Participating in class, doing homework, studying for classroom tests or doing well on the PSAE are not in alignment with their personal life expectations.

*"I am African American and I see many other African Americans like me always blaming others for everything. It is always somebody else's fault. It makes me sad because I know that we as a race can do a lot better, as good as White people or Asian people, if we try. They say that the teachers are racist or the school is racist and all that. I know that there are a lot of racist people everywhere; but I don't think that's the real reason why they don't do well in school. They like to play the 'race card.'"*

*"There is a very easy solution to this complex problem. That solution is responsibility! Responsibility is a hard pill to swallow, but, it is the perfect remedy. Parents are responsible for mentoring their children. Teachers are responsible for actually caring about their students' performance and not accepting Ds as satisfactory. Students are responsible for not taking the easy way out and saying. 'Oh, I'm Black or I'm Hispanic and the world expects me to fail, so I'll fail.' These simply are duties that cannot be shirked."*

# FINDING # 6

## Students have low academic expectations for themselves.

*African American and Hispanic Students/Level of Intensity:*
*HIGH*

Both African American and Hispanic students regularly expressed that their same-race/ethnic peers have low academic expectations for themselves. Many of these students do not believe that they have the potential to achieve academic success. This lack of faith in their potential significantly correlates with past failures in school, over-representation in lower-track academic subjects, low performance on standardized tests, and parents' low academic expectations.

*"I feel that African Americans don't try because they are fine with settling for an 'ok' grade. They feel like if the grade causes them not to graduate, then they should try. If it's the other way around, then, they don't care if it's a D or F. That is ridiculous to me because as an African American myself, I feel that I should be trying my hardest to prove statistics wrong. We should expect more from us! They are throwing away their future and heading down a path that does not bring joy at*

*all. They are making Civil Rights leaders look like fools. Martin Luther King Jr. worked hard for us to have an equal education. He died because he wanted the future to be better for the African American community. It's like we are spitting in the face of every African American activist."*

*"I feel that Hispanic students don't think they can accomplish a lot because they think they can't. They don't see many Hispanics in honors classes or taking AP courses. I am the only one in my AP Calculus class. It is hard for me because I am the only Hispanic there. Most Hispanics don't graduate or just graduate and then work in McDonalds or something like that. I think Hispanics don't expect to achieve high because they think that they are different from White and Asian students. They don't think they can do well in school and go to college."*

# FINDING # 7

## Students exhibit behaviors that are not conducive to academic success.

*African American and Hispanic Students/Level of Intensity:*
*HIGH*

Many African American and Hispanic students stated that their same-race/ethnic peers were underachieving due to engaging in behaviors that are not conducive to academic success. African American and Hispanic students are more likely than White and Asian students to:

1. Be late to class, skip class or miss school.
2. Not participate in class, do homework, or study for the tests.
3. Be involved in gang activity and/or alcohol/drug abuse.

*"I think that our scores are lower because of the media. They (students) want to be 'ghetto-fabulous' and they want to be considered 'street.' They don't do homework or read books because they want to be like the media says we are. I see that many*

*African American students and Hispanics too, are late to class or miss school all together because they think it's cool to do all that. That's why they are always in trouble. We, as a people, need to get rid of trying to be thug and pretending that it's a cool thing to be because it's not. I am Black but I know that there are no opportunities for the future that way."*

*"A large percent of these races (African-American and Hispanic) are involved in other activities such as gangs and they don't take education so serious. Most of the kids that I know are involved in gangs and they don't take education as a big task in life. You really don't see many White and Asians being in gangs. I think if there were less gang activities we would have a larger percent of students doing good in school and in tests."*

*"Americans want to succeed. But, Mexicans, they just want to be involved in drugs and gangs and all that. Good kids, they actually study and do well in school. But, as soon as they get involved in drugs and stuff, they start doing poorly. Because I think they just want to fit in."*

# FINDING # 8

**Students exhibit disruptive classroom behaviors in English as a Second Language (ESL) and/or Bilingual classes.**

*Hispanic Students/Level of Intensity: MEDIUM*

Some Hispanic students expressed that many ELL students exhibit poor behavior in ESL and/or Bilingual classes. These students reported that their peers display an excessive amount of disruptive behavior that is not conducive to learning. These behaviors seem to be more prevalent in classes taught by Caucasian teachers than in classes taught by Hispanic teachers. Students interviewed indicated that Caucasian teachers tend to be more concerned about helping students feel accepted than enforcing classroom discipline. They also suggested that these same ELL students exhibit appropriate behaviors in classes in which they were a minority such as art, band, physical education, etc.

*"In classes of Hispanics or in Shelter, where there are pure Hispanics, I think that there is a lot of playing around. Because, what Hispanics like is to play around.*

*Those who like to pay attention should not go with the flow. Because we are 'relajistas' and all that, we just go with the flow like the rest. I think Hispanic percentages do not improve because the small numbers who make an effort and want to achieve at the end give up."*

*"It is all fooling around in the ESL and Bilingual classes. It is all talking and passing notes and whatever else to distract others. But, I see those same kids behaving really good in the other classes, like art or Driver's Ed. I guess it is because most of the kids there are not Hispanics and everything is in English."*

*"I think that many bilingual kids do not pay attention to the teachers and do not prepare well for the tests. For example, I have seen many students in my ESL class that when the teacher is explaining things they are listening to music or doing other things and not paying attention to the teacher, maybe most of the guys. If the teacher is Hispanic, they behave better because she understands all the jokes and all the words, even the bad ones."*

# FINDING # 9

## Students live for the present and need immediate gratification.

*African American/Level of Intensity:  HIGH*

A significant number of African American students expressed that for many of their same-race peers, doing homework, studying for tests and participating in class did not provide the immediate gratification they needed. Good students understand that they reap the benefits of academic success in the future. Today's society prompts many of their peers to expect immediate gratification rather than plan for their future.

*"The reason for the huge gap that exists between the scores of White and Asian students and those of Hispanic and African American students is that Blacks want everything right now and they never plan ahead for the future. They are also more concerned with the leisurely and insignificant things in life such as which music video landed on the number one spot on MTV (Music Television) or who is in first place in the AL (American League) East division in baseball.  On the other hand, Asian and White students have a higher, more visible level of work ethic and*

*determination. They believe that if they work hard now, it will only pay off later in the future."*

*"If Hispanics and African-American could focus more on a future goal instead of just thinking about the present, they would definitely improve on test scores because they will have a goal in mind. I think that since the Hispanic and African American students do not have that many role models, they need more guidance towards setting goals for themselves."*

*"I always see that the kids that have goals and study hard are White. It is the same thing with the Asians. They study hard because they want to have a career. Me too, but most Blacks and Hispanics want things that make them happy now. It is hard for them to think about the future. Maybe it is because they have a hard life or maybe they don't have hope or maybe no one at home is pushing them to do well in school."*

# FINDING # 10

## Students already feel successful.

*Hispanic Students/Level of Intensity: MEDIUM*

Some Hispanic students expressed that many of their same-ethnic peers, especially those who have recently arrived in the United States, feel a sense of success based upon meeting basic goals. For many of them, merely being in the United States is the fulfillment of a lifetime aspiration. They now hold part-time jobs where they earn more than their parents earned in their native countries. They will soon graduate from high school, making them the first in their families to accomplish this feat. This sense of accomplishment does not motivate these students to pursue higher academic goals.

*"For me, being here in the United States it is like being born again. It is like a dream come true - a new opportunity that life has given me. I speak English and I already make more money than my parents did back in Mexico. I will be the first in my family to graduate. When I someday go back, they (family and friends in Mexico) will see the difference."*

41

*"I live with my mother, uncle, aunt, and little brother. We are five people and I am the oldest one. I have to put an example to him. None of my relatives have even got to the high school level. They have started high school but dropped out. None of them has actually made it. I will be the first one to graduate high school and I have to live up to their expectations."*

*"I always wanted to be in the United States since I was little. So, I am here now. I am helping my parents and I will graduate from high school."*

*"For me to graduate high school will change my life because I want to get ahead, work, earn money, help my parents and get out of all these problems."*

# FINDING # 11

## Students fear same-race/ethnic rejection.

*African American and Hispanic Students/Level of Intensity: HIGH*

African American and Hispanic students who behave according to mainstream behavioral norms risk being ostracized by their same-race/ethnic peers. There was consensus among the students interviewed that behaving in an ethnically correct manner deters many of their same-race/ethnic peers from meeting their academic potential. Doing homework, studying for classroom tests, participating in class, etc. are often interpreted as "acting White" or "acting güero." Students must choose between peer acceptance by or socially isolated from their same-race/ethnic peers.

*"The friends we may have could be telling us, 'Man, why are you doing all that? Why don't you chill with us? As for us Blacks, I think that we should try not to put each other down but up. If we do things the right way, then the other Blacks say that we 'acting White.' It is hard for me because most of the students in this school*

*are White, not like in the city. Black students should know that we are not 'acting White' at all, but just want to get somewhere in life. So, if we do right, we could be by ourselves and be alone."*

*"Hispanics think that we have to behave in a certain way. If I get good grades and participate in school clubs and things like that, they make fun of me and say, 'Oh, look at her. She thinks she is a 'güera!' I have White friends and some Asian friends too. But, I would like other Hispanics to accept me too because I am a Latina and will always be a Latina."*

*"I feel like I have to choose. If I do homework, participate in class and have good grades, then I can't hang out with the other Hispanics in school. I want to be with my own race but it is like I don't belong there either. So, I am like in the middle. I am not White but I want to do well in school."*

# FINDING # 12

## Students are undocumented.

*Hispanic Students/Level of Intensity:  HIGH*

Many Hispanic students stated that one reason their same-ethnic peers are doing poorly in school and on the PSAE is that they are not legal residents. Undocumented students cannot obtain a U.S. social security number. Without a social security number, students cannot hold a driver's license, legally hold a part-time job, nor qualify for Federal financial aid. It is the belief of the respondents that undocumented students who overcome these challenges and manage to earn a post-secondary degree will never reap the benefits of that post-secondary education.  With or without a degree, employers cannot legally hire someone who lacks a social security number. According to the students, "No matter how well they do in school, they are sentenced to live a life in the shadows."

*"I think that not being in this country legally has a big negative effect. The purpose of studying and achieving good grades is to obtain a good and well-paying job and for that you need to have 'papers' (legal residency). Most of those (students) who come to*

*school and don't do well, is because they do not have papers and are only attending (school) because their parents make them and they have to come to school. They (undocumented students) know they are not going any place when they leave high school. It does not matter to them if they do well on exams that help them go to college."*

*"What can you do if you are illegal? Nothing! You just exist. Why should I bother to do homework, study for tests and all that if at the end it will not make any difference? I came when I was a baby. If I am deported, what am I going to do there (Mexico)? It is so unfair. I wish at least I could have an ID!"*

*"I have been treated differently not because of my race but because I'm illegal. One of my friends actually stopped talking to me because he found out I was illegal. I get stereotyped, even by teachers. I can tell when they think I'm not worth the time. After a while, I start doing my work but with very little effort. Students call me 'wetback,' 'beaner,' and 'spick.' It is very hard to work hard when you do not have papers."*

# FINDING # 13

## Students have other responsibilities at home.

*Hispanic Students/Level of Intensity: HIGH*

Hispanic students consistently articulated that responsibilities at home prevent their same-ethnic peers from achieving greater academic success. Many Hispanic high school students miss school to interpret for their parents, take care of their younger siblings, and/or hold part-time jobs to help support their families. These responsibilities impede students from preparing for class, completing homework assignments, studying for tests and participating in extra-curricular activities.

*"The main reason why Hispanic students don't do well in school and have low test scores is their families. Hispanics worry more about supporting their families and helping their parents as opposed to White people. Most Hispanics work and have to take care of their siblings and do not have much time to deal with schoolwork."*

*"I always have to help my parents interpreting for them. Sometimes, my dad has to go to court or my mom needs to see the doctor. Sometimes, I hate it because I have to miss school or a test. Then I have to catch up and it is more difficult for me."*

*"I have to work a lot to help my parents. I love them and I see how much they work to support us. I have a pretty decent GPA, but I have to work very hard to maintain it. My sister, who will graduate in two years, has to babysit almost every day. We don't mind because family is important. But, teachers don't understand that we are not like the White kids. We have other things to do."*

*"I would like to stay after school and participate in many of the activities they have here in this school. There is a lot going on when school is over. My teachers are always asking me why I don't stay so I can participate. They don't understand that I have to go home and take care of my baby sister so my mom can go to work."*

# FINDING # 14

## Students live in home environments that are not conducive to academic success.

*African American and Hispanic Students/Level of Intensity: HIGH*

A significant number of both African American and Hispanic students believe that their same-race/ethnic peers are likely to live in home environments that are not conducive to academic success. According to students, these home environments are characterized by limited financial resources, lack of parental supervision, constant distractions, crowded living conditions, etc. The students spend a significant amount of time unsupervised because the adults in their lives are working and/or preoccupied with other matters. All their efforts are concentrated in simply trying to make ends meet. Sharing limited home space with other relatives creates crowded conditions and constant distractions. Some Hispanic students reported living with relatives because their parents were in their native countries. These home circumstances do not provide students with the structure, discipline, accountability, etc., needed to excel in school and maintain behaviors that are conducive to academic success.

*"Home life plays a big role in these two ethnicities. Many Hispanic students as well as African American students grow up having a tough life. Often times their parents work for long hours, and this causes the parents to not have enough time to supervise their children and focus on their education."*

*"Many times the parents are in Mexico so students do not have support from their parents. In my case, I come to school every day and also work to send them (parents) money."*

*"African Americans sometimes do not have that many resources because they simply do not have enough money to pay for it all. They are all stressed out and worried. So they don't pay too much attention to their kids' education."*

*"Many times Hispanics live in small places because they don't have the money to pay for something bigger. Many times their relatives live with them because they don't have a place to stay. For example, I have to share my room with my cousins and my aunt. It gets really crowded and everything gets really complicated. It is hard to study with so many people."*

*"In most Hispanic families there is loud music and blaring TV with the 'novellas.' The parents, or whoever, are talking really loud or always on the phone talking to relatives. I think the same happens in the homes of Black students. There are too many distractions going on. Who can study like that?"*

# FINDING # 15

## Parents have a limited academic background and/or lack English proficiency.

*Hispanic Students/Level of Intensity: HIGH*

Consensus was reached among Hispanic students that one of the reasons for their same-ethnic peers' poor performance in school is their parents' limited academic background and/or lack of English proficiency. They reported having higher levels of education and English proficiency than their parents. Many of their parents have not graduated from high school or finished their secondary education in their native countries. They also stated that their parents have difficulty understanding English and could neither read nor write it. By the time they reach high school, they stated that they are primarily responsible for their own education. Their parents could not comprehend the challenges they face, adequately monitor their education nor assist them regarding which courses to take, how to prepare for college entrance tests or how to apply for financial aid.

"My parents expect so much from me and continuously tell me that I need to do well in school because that is why they sacrificed it all to come here. But, they are completely clueless as to what my school experience is like because they didn't get as far as I did. In Mexico, they finished like in middle school. They want to help but they can't. Hispanic students struggle a lot because they are pretty much on their own."

"I prefer not to give my parents all those papers that the school sends home. It is hard for me because I have to translate everything. It takes a lot of time! So, I cannot expect them to help me nor to tell me what to do. I have to figure things out by myself, like which college to go to and what to do to get Financial Aid."

"White students, and also Asians, have their parents backing them in everything. They have their parents coaching them, always telling them what to do to move ahead. They know what to do to help their kids. White and Asian kids are always worried about their grades because their parents know how to go online and check. I know how to go online and check, but my parents don't."

# FINDING # 16

## Parents have low academic expectations.

*African American and Hispanic Students/Level of Intensity: HIGH*

Both African American and Hispanic students consistently reported that many of their parents do not expect them to earn a high GPA, enroll in rigorous academic subjects or pursue a college career after graduating from high school. According to these students, their parents are content if their children simply attend school, pass their classes and graduate high school.

*"It has a lot to do with the parents. White students' parents are involved in their students' education. They care a lot about their grades. In my case, my parents are satisfied if I get a C, as long as I pass the class. Hispanic parents care, but not that much. They do not expect their kids to try as hard as they should. Most Hispanic parents have lower expectations. White parents make their children work harder, they want the best. They are not satisfied with a C."*

*"Parents need to see the importance of their child's education. They need to set higher expectations. They need to have punishments for not doing the homework, for not passing tests, or being late to class. Also, I think if parents really get involved in their child's education they will get to the point where they will set rewards for getting an A or maybe a bigger reward if they get A+. I know that worked for me. But, many Black and Hispanic students don't have that."*

*"I think that a lot of Hispanics and Blacks don't do well because of their parents. In my case, I don't try so hard to do well in school because my parents are not expecting me to go to college or anything like that. They just want me to graduate so I can work and help out."*

# FINDING # 17

## Parents do not understand the American Educational System.

*Hispanic Students/Level of Intensity: HIGH*

Hispanics students consistently believed that one of the greatest reasons for their lack of academic achievement is their parents' lack of understanding of the American educational system. This deficit does not allow parents to monitor their children's education. Students, especially at the high school level, reported being on their own regarding their academic careers.

*"My parents want the best for me. They want me to get a good education. But, they don't know anything about how the school works. The school system in Mexico is very different. They don't have a test like the PSAE. Even the grades are different."*

*"One thing with the whole parent issue is that maybe parents can be given some understanding of our education. My parents don't understand the school system and they don't know how to know. Schools should teach our parents how to help us in*

*any way they can because their help can make a big impact in our lives. You know, in many cases, they are our biggest influence in life."*

*"White students get a lot of help from their parents. Their parents went to school here, and they know a lot of stuff about school and what to do to go to college. Hispanics have to explain everything to their parents."*

# FINDING # 18

## Teachers and administrators have low academic expectations.

*African American and Hispanic Students/Level of Intensity: HIGH*

Both African American and Hispanic students frequently reported that many of their teachers expect little from them academically. According to these students, their teachers' low academic expectations are fueled by their same-race/ethic peers' under-representation in courses that prepare students for college, low performance on the PSAE and other college entrance tests, and parents' lack of involvement in their children's education.

*"Teachers need to be stricter and expect more out of Black and Hispanic students. They must push, push and push."*

*"If you are Hispanic, teachers don't really expect you to do well. I know that because I see it. Most Hispanic students just take the easy classes. Their grades are not that good either. So, teachers are not expecting too much from them. I feel like I*

*have to prove to them (teachers) that I care about my grades. We are not all the same. I want to have a career and have a good life. Some teachers are surprised. I think teachers should know that we are not all the same."*

*"African American students score lower than their peers (White and Asian students) because there are no real expectations for them to succeed coming from the administration, in general. It is still a stereotype that Black students don't care about their high school education and it is a hard stereotype to break free from. This instills in them the mentality that they won't succeed despite their efforts, so why bother trying?"*

# FINDING # 19

## Teachers do not seem to care about their students' education.

*African American and Hispanic Students/Level of Intensity: HIGH*

Many African American and Hispanic students stated that some of their teachers simply do not care about their education. It is their belief that these teachers do not have a love of or passion for teaching. They feel these teachers do their job out of economic necessity, not due to a concern for students.

*"Personally, I think it's not about the test scores alone, but about the school itself. Many kids are looking for support at school because they don't receive it at home. Teachers here do not care! They don't push for their students to strive for the best; they don't encourage the minorities to make things seem attainable such as going to college and pursuing their dreams. Many of the faculty and staff pay attention to the wrong students, the ones who are succeeding and making the grades they need. I believe they need to be paying attention to the ones who sit in the back of the*

*classroom, the ones who don't turn in their work. They (teachers) just end up labeling these kids as bad students. Basically, teachers need to be more involved with their students."*

*"Teachers have to care more. Students are surrounded by teachers for more than 6 hours a day, 5 times a week. If a student does not understand something, stop and take the time to review. In many math classes, students are flying through the material. Students are not learning; they are simply trying to remember how to do it. I think they (teachers) do that because they do not care."*

*"The teachers need to be resourceful. A lot of teachers say that they don't stay after school because they don't get paid for it. It's sad to hear that. When I hear a teacher saying that, I get so mad. It makes me feel like that teacher is just here for the money. I want to hear from teachers that they want to stay after school because they care about us and that they love what they teach."*

# FINDING # 20

## Teachers demonstrate a negative attitude toward the PSAE.

*African American and Hispanic Students/Level of Intensity: LOW*

A small number of students from both groups disclosed that their teachers express frustration with the NCLB Act, Adequate Yearly Progress (AYP) requirements and the PSAE during class time. Teachers are not motivated to prepare students for a test they consider to be an unfair measure of teachers' and students' performances. Teachers are being held accountable for a test that measures more than a decade of accumulated learning. According to these students, it is very difficult to prepare for a test that is not supported by their teachers.

*"I think this school really has a good set of teachers. The problem is that the Federal government believes that they know what we should know. That's the problem! I agree with some of my teachers that it should be up to the school to decide*

*what we need to know and how we should all learn it. Teachers can't do their own plans about what they want us to learn because of the PSAE. I think that the standardized testing is causing a problem in how teachers are performing and filters down on how students are performing."*

*"I agree with my teachers. The PSAE is hurting us all. The school has a bad reputation because of it. It also makes us, Hispanics, look bad because we don't do that well. For example, many Hispanics were not born here and they don't read English that well. I agree with my teacher. It is not fair that they (ELL students) have to take the test. We have a lot of bilingual kids in this school."*

*"It is a waste of time doing all those worksheets to prepare for the test. Teachers don't want to do it. They do it because the administration forces them to do it. At the end, if they don't want to do it, they are not going to do a good job."*

# FINDING # 21

## Students attend schools that lack staff diversity.

*African American and Hispanic Students/Level of Intensity: HIGH*

Both African American and Hispanic students consistently expressed that their schools' professional staff members do not proportionally reflect their own race or ethnicity. Not seeing African American or Hispanic teachers, counselors, social workers, etc. working in their schools has a negative impact in the way they view themselves. It is the students' belief that the mainstream Caucasian staff members do not have the knowledge and insights to help minority students overcome the personal and school-related challenges they face on a daily basis.

*"First, I think that the Board of Education should have an evenly mixed board so that no one would feel like the schools are being racist. There should be a few African American counselors, so that Black students can have someone that they can relate to when they need to talk to someone."*

*"In order for Hispanics to improve, the school has to make drastic changes. I believe the school should start off by hiring more Hispanic teachers. If they hire more Hispanic teachers, the students will feel comfortable and will have someone there who understands them. The students will also see that a Hispanic person can make it and have a career."*

*"There are a lot of really good White teachers in my school. I like them and everything but I feel they do not understand what I go through. It is hard to be a minority. There is only one Black teacher. Could you believe that?"*

*"I think there should be classes for teachers to understand different cultures. That way the teachers can understand what minorities go through on a daily basis. They will understand how to deal with our situations and understand the way we feel."*

# FINDING # 22

## Students feel they do not belong to the school culture.

*African American and Hispanic Students/Level of Intensity: HIGH*

A significant number of African American and Hispanic students perceived a cultural mismatch between themselves and their schools' cultures - causing them to feel marginalized. According to these students, it is very difficult to excel in a school environment in which they do not feel included or welcomed. This lack of comfort is more evident among African American students who transfer from Chicago Public Schools (CPS) or Hispanic students who were born and spent a portion of their lives in Latin America.

*"When Hispanic students see all other heritages being recognized, they tend to feel left out and believe they are not important. Hispanics and African-Americans are also the minorities in schools. Therefore, they feel as if they do not belong and do not have the ability to succeed like the majority. When a student knows that someone believes they can achieve great things, they begin to believe in themselves. And, when*

*students believe in themselves, they try harder. I believe once the schools start to set a good example to all the students, they will see a change in the scores, not only in the PSAE, but in every educational department."*

*"I think we are different. I mean, we speak Spanish at home and do things differently. When I was in in elementary school, back in Mexico, I felt like everyone else. It was fun to be in school. Now I feel like I don't belong here. We are a minority here. And I think the administration does not really like us because we are immigrants."*

*"We moved to the suburbs because we had to. My mom also said that the schools are better here. The schools in the city are really bad, but not all of them. Most of the students in this school are White. I don't have anything against White people but I don't feel I fit in. There are few Blacks and some Hispanics. There are some Asian kids and they always do well in all their classes. I think that Blacks and Hispanics don't do well because we are different."*

# FINDING # 23

## Schools are culturally biased or racist.

*African American and Hispanic Students/Level of Intensity:*
*MEDIUM*

Some students, both African American and Hispanic, reported that some of their schools' staff members demonstrate biased or racist behaviors. It is these students' beliefs that they are more likely to find themselves in trouble with the school authorities than White or Asian students. They stated that their teachers' negative feelings regarding African American and Hispanic students are fueled by their own over representation in lower-track academic subjects and poor performance on the PSAE. Their same-race/ethnic peers are also more likely to receive detentions, be suspended, or be expelled from school for behaviors that are not conducive to academic success.

*"I know that when a whole bunch of White kids hang out in the halls no one says anything. But, if the Hispanics do the same thing then they get in trouble. I think the administration thinks Hispanics are all gang members. And also, if we speak in Spanish, teachers think we are saying bad things about them. And, then we get*

*in trouble. I guess they think that way because of everything they see happening with Hispanics in the media."*

*"We, as a whole, are stereotyped and designed to fail. If possible, the whole system is designed to fail all African Americans instead of making them successful. Don't get me wrong, I am not blaming it all on the school administrations and the government. I will accept that we Blacks have also failed."*

*"As a high school student and as an African American I have seen and been through a lot. I have been called names. I have heard every kind of racial slur you can possibly think. For instance, in my gym class, a teacher said something that really upset me very much. We were just starting the basketball season and he pulled me and said: 'Oh you, you should be good at basketball. You are Black.' It's almost like a natural thing. What is that supposed to mean? Don't get me wrong. I am proud of African Americans being able to play basketball. But, was that necessary to point me out in front of the whole class and say that kind of stuff?"*

# FINDING # 24

## There is too much government assistance or a sense of entitlement.

*African American Students/Level of Intensity: MEDIUM*

Some African American students expressed that there is a sense of entitlement among their same-race peers. There are some African American students that were raised in an environment in which the government provided for their basic needs such as housing, food and health care. Based on this premise, there is no need to put a great amount of effort into achieving academic success when their needs will be met by the government. In spite of a poor academic outcome, they will have their needs met for them.

*"African Americans in my opinion are 'babied' a lot by the government. Most of the African American communities receive welfare from the government. Receiving welfare takes their motivation off when it comes to working and receiving a higher education."*

*"The government only wants the Blacks to depend on food stamps and Medicaid. Instead of giving us food stamps, why not provide us with a job or an opportunity for us to go to school?"*

*"Many Black students know that they will have a roof and food no matter what. So, there is no big reason why to sacrifice today for a better future. It feels good today but at the long run it will hurt us."*

*"Minorities are used to getting help from the government. I used to see that in my neighborhood all the time before I moved here. We don't really have to work hard because if we don't and fail in life, we will always survive. It is like the government owes us and they have to pay no matter what."*

# FINDING # 25

## People have negative opinions regarding Hispanics.

*Hispanic Students/Level of Intensity: HIGH*

Hispanic students believe that the mainstream culture's negative opinion regarding Hispanics represents a barrier to their academic success. Many Hispanic students expressed that it is very difficult to excel in school when they belong to an ethnic group with such a negative stigma. The national media, according to these students, is fueling an anti-illegal immigration sentiment and there is a tendency to associate the term Hispanic with an illegal immigration status. In general, people do not have a positive opinion about Hispanics because Hispanics are more likely to live in poverty, do poorly in school, and participate in anti-social behaviors.

*"All you hear in the media is bad, like crossing the border and doing all kinds of bad things. Sometimes they think we are taking their jobs. That is so stupid. No one wants to do the work we do."*

*"Society has already marked us (Hispanics) as being incapable to do something in our lives other than working in construction or McDonald's. All those ideas can stick to your mind and you lose hope for a better future. So, if you don't have hope, you don't have any reason why to study hard and do your best."*

*"They think because you are Hispanic then you are illegal. I was born here but they think all Mexicans are illegal and should not be here."*

*"My friends always told me that before they knew me they were scared of me. They did not want to talk to me and were afraid I might get mad and beat them up. They criticized me because they were being ignorant. They think all Hispanics love to fight."*

# RECOMMENDATIONS

# RECOMMENDATIONS

## What the DuPage Regional Office of Education Endorses

The following 27 recommendations are offered as possible pathways for improving the academic achievement of African American and Hispanic students. They are not presented in a specific order; all have the potential to be high priorities depending on the unique needs of students and their schools.

Some of the recommendations are intended to create awareness among school staff members regarding cultural nuances that could deter students from academic success. Awareness can be a catalyst for improving student-staff relationships that lead to greater student academic achievement.

Other recommendations are intended to serve as criteria for selecting future professional development opportunities. Professional development can provide the knowledge and skills needed to effectively teach or work with students from diverse backgrounds.

Last, but not least, we offer recommendations to jump start school/district-wide initiatives to create/modify curriculums, create/modify school programs and launch/participate in student activities.

# RECOMMENDATION # 1

## Teach parents and students the value of education, starting in the elementary grades.

Teachers and school administrators must refrain from assuming that parents are instilling the value of education in their children. There are numerous African American and Hispanic students who are growing up in homes where education is not embraced. For example, some Hispanic parents might perceive work, not education, as the pathway to a better future. Some African American parents might have a frame of reference in which educational attainment is external or alien to their realm of subjective realities.

We recommend that schools proactively and consistently teach parents and students, at all grade levels, the intrinsic long-term value of education and the personal, family and community benefits that it provides. These messages can be delivered during instructional time, in-school and out-of-school encounters, or during parent and community events. We recommend that greater efforts be focused on students and their families starting at the elementary grades. Elementary school students have less distortion and misinformation regarding education to unlearn.

# RECOMMENDATION # 2

## Implement school-wide initiatives to increase parental involvement.

Parent involvement is one of the leading indicators of student academic achievement. Research indicates that many African-American and Hispanic parents are not involved in their children's education the way teachers expect and need them to be.

Some Hispanic parents believe that the teacher is the expert. Therefore, they relinquish all responsibility regarding their children's education to the teacher. There are also Hispanic parents who simply do not understand how the American educational system works and others who lack the English language skills needed to effectively communicate with school staff.

Some African American parents feel disenfranchised from the public school system. These parents experience a level of discomfort or mistrust in dealing with administrators or teachers in schools where the White middle class is the majority. Additionally, many of these parents still struggle with an intra-psyche battle: either they embrace academic rigor or, in lieu of being perceived as "acting White," they settle for generational academic failure.

It is for these reasons that we recommend that every school assigns and trains school staff members to facilitate a yearly series of culturally-sensitive and relevant parent involvement workshops. Using adult education best practices, these workshops can be delivered during week evenings or on Saturday mornings. As a part of these workshops, parents must learn how to:

1. Read and interpret their children's standardized test reports (ISAT, PSAE, ACT, ACCESS, STAR, etc.)

2. Help their children reach grade-level reading and mathematics proficiencies.

3. Make homework completion part of their children's daily routine.

4. Connect with their children's teachers in a positive and productive manner.

5. Build in their children's lives the character traits that are conducive to academic success such as responsibility, persistence, a strong work ethic and the ability to delay their personal gratification.

# RECOMMENDATION # 3

## Operate from the belief system that every student can learn.

Research shows that students often rise to the level of teachers' expectations. Beliefs drive behaviors. Teachers who believe students can learn will expect them to learn and achieve academic expectations. Teachers who believe that the students do not have the potential to achieve academic success often lower their standards, which can result in minimal or mediocre levels of academic performance.

We must reject the notion that some students are academically capable while others are not. We recommend that school administrators do whatever is in their power to ensure that teachers not only believe, but also communicate to their students that proficiency in any academic subject can be reached through commitment, focus, effort, obtaining feedback, and the formulation of strategies for improvement based on the feedback.

# RECOMMENDATION # 4

## Provide students with a pathway for improving their reading and mathematics skills.

Nationwide data shows that, beginning with their enrollment in elementary school, many African American and Hispanic students perform significantly below grade level in both reading and mathematics. This has translated into persistent academic achievement gaps between these students and their White and Asian peers - gaps that are likely to widen at the high school level. Students who lack proficiency in reading and mathematics are far more likely to drop out of school, do poorly on college entrance tests, fail college-level courses, and have a difficult time finding and maintaining a job.

Because classroom instruction alone is not likely to help students reach grade-level proficiency, we recommend that schools provide during- and after-school opportunities for students to increase their levels of reading comprehension and mathematical skills. Regardless of the subject area, and especially at the middle and high school levels, the school administrators must inform teachers about students' reading and mathematics proficiency levels. The earlier these deficiencies are identified and abated, the greater the chances are for students to meet grade-level academic expectations.

# RECOMMENDATION # 5

## Accelerate ELL high school students' English language acquisition.

It is an uphill battle to attain a quality life in a country where you have not mastered the language. Hispanic immigrant students who enroll in U.S. schools at the high school level have four or fewer years to not only meet graduation requirements, but also to reach English language proficiency. They will have difficulty succeeding in a post-secondary educational program or finding and retaining a job if they do not understand, speak, read, and write English at an adequate level of proficiency.

We recommend that school administrators and ESL/Bilingual coordinators ensure that these students have sufficient access to mainstream academic courses. It is educationally beneficial for ELL students to be in courses that are taught in English where most students are either mainstreamed Hispanics or native English speakers. Research shows that the most effective way to learn a second language is within a curricular context. Participation in mainstream courses also provides ELL students with an opportunity to practice English by communicating with their peers. Building relationships with mainstream students can also accelerate the process of acculturation.

.

# RECOMMENDATION # 6

## Learn strategies that increase the comprehensibility of the English language.

Teachers and support staff members must realize that some Hispanic students might not fully understand everything they hear in English, either during class or other encounters. This is especially true with newly-arrived students or those who started their education in a Spanish-speaking country. These students frequently encounter new English words, phrases, sayings, etc. when they are exposed to a new context or a new situation. A foreign accent or syntax mistakes should not be the only criteria for assuming or determining a lack of English language proficiency. Students who may appear fluent in English might not fully comprehend the intended message. For example, the saying "survival of the fittest" might be misunderstood as "survival of the fetus." To an ELL student "fittest" and "fetus" may sound the same.

We recommend that school staff members, who have direct contact with Hispanic students, receive training in how to interpret students' body language and facial expressions to determine their level of language comprehension. Then, they must learn strategies to communicate more effectively with native Spanish-speakers. Using body language, paraphrasing or supporting verbal or written communication with visuals can augment the students' opportunity for grasping the correct meaning.

# RECOMMENDATION # 7

## Learn how Hispanic students progress through the multiple stages of acculturation.

The first-generation or foreign-born Hispanic students who enroll in U.S. schools are faced with the reality of navigating a culture they do not know or understand. To achieve academic success, these students will not only need to learn the language, but also the beliefs, values, norms, etc. of the American mainstream culture – a process known as acculturation. Acculturation is a multi-year process defined by the following four stages:

a.  "Honeymoon"
b.  Cultural Shock
c.  Cultural Stress
d.  Adaptation

To assist students with this critical process, we recommend that school administrators and staff members, who have contact with first-generation Hispanic students, enroll in training in which they can learn about the challenges first-generation Hispanic students face during the stages of acculturation. This will help minimize miscommunication between students and teachers. During these trainings, administrators and staff members must also learn strategies to help students and their families gently climb the transition ladder leading to biculturalism.

# RECOMMENDATION # 8

## Learn how Hispanic students progress through the process of language acquisition.

Hispanic immigrant students who enroll in U.S. schools are challenged with the reality of having to learn a new language. To succeed academically, they must be proficient in English. Experts in the field of language acquisition state that reaching language proficiency is a multi-year process defined by the following five stages:

a. Pre-production or the "Silent Period"
b. Early Production
c. Speech Emergence
d. Intermediate Fluency
e. Advanced Fluency

To assist students with this critical process, we recommend that school administrators and staff members who have or are likely to have direct contact with first-generation Hispanic students enroll in training to learn about the challenges students face during the stages of language acquisition, thus minimizing the possibilities for student-teacher miscommunication. During these trainings school administrators and staff members must also learn strategies to accelerate the students' English language acquisition.

.

# RECOMMENDATION # 9

**Implement strategies to increase minority students' enrollment in advanced courses and participation in extra-curricular school activities.**

Research shows that there is a positive correlation between the courses that students take in high school and their performance on college entrance tests. A rigorous curricular program leads to better test scores and performance in any post-secondary program. It is an accepted notion that African American and Hispanic students are less likely to enroll in advanced course work. Because of this, they are more likely to do poorly on college entrance tests and are forced to enroll in remedial courses at the college level.

Extra-curricular activities can keep students off the streets and out of trouble. The participation of minority students in after-school programs can also create a sense of belonging, provide opportunities to relate to students from different backgrounds, and offer life skills such as self-discipline, teamwork, leadership, etc.

To accomplish these goals, the administration must assign staff members who understand the underlying reasons for the students' lack of participation in either higher track academic courses and/or extra-curricular activities. These staff members must have the ability to connect with the students and persuade them to overcome their resistance to participation.

# RECOMMENDATION # 10

**Increase staff awareness regarding the values, beliefs, perceptions, attitudes, etc. of the American mainstream culture.**

It is common knowledge that U.S.A. is steadily becoming a more racially and ethnically diverse country. This national trend has created the need for our citizens to develop a better understanding of the American mainstream culture. Consequently, it is important that educators understand the values, beliefs, attitudes, and perceptions of who we are as people of this nation before we try to reach out to students from other cultures.

Ift is for this reason that we recommend that school administrators and staff members who work in highly diverse schools engage in professional development courses that provide the opportunity to discuss and analyze the cultural components that are at the heart of the American mainstream culture. These components include freedom of expression, self-actualization, upward mobility, equal opportunity, a strong work ethic, accountability, respect for time, etc.

It is our belief that the better we understand ourselves as Americans, the better we can help students from diverse cultural backgrounds understand and embrace American mainstream culture.

# RECOMMENDATION # 11

**Advocate for professional development opportunities that promote cultural competence among school staff members.**

As schools and school districts increase in diversity, the need to relate to people from a variety of cultural backgrounds becomes ever-more critical. Cultural competence is a conduit through which people from different backgrounds can work together to pursue common goals. In the education arena, cultural competence includes practices that build bridges of understanding between culturally-diverse students and practitioners of the mainstream culture. It is also an approach that requires the inclusion of diverse perspectives in the administrative process in a manner that validates and affirms students from marginalized groups. School staffs that are trained in and embrace cultural competence are more likely to:

1. Differentiate instruction, counseling, etc.
2. Build authentic relationships with students, parents, etc.

3. Make instruction relevant to the students.

4. Become positive agents of change, which will hopefully lead to higher student academic success.

It is essential that, during cultural competence trainings, participants develop the comfort level needed to engage in courageous conversations so that they are able to share sensitive information about race, ethnicity, language, isolation, immigration status, etc.

# RECOMMENDATION # 12

## Take a holistic approach to learning about students.

We often know our students' names, race or ethnicity, classroom demeanors and their academic performances. However, there is more to our students than meets the eye. The more we know about our students the better we are able establish authentic student-teacher relationships that are predicated on mutual respect.

According to Dr. Stanley Greenspan, "There is no significant learning without a significant relationship." Therefore, we strongly recommend that teachers, and any other staff members who have direct contact with African American and Hispanic students, spend time, especially at the beginning of the school year, looking beyond their students' initial presentations. We advise that school staff learn more about their students' countries of origin, the languages they speak, with whom they live, the sports they play, the hobbies they have, their goals in life, and the challenges they face in school, home, and life.

# RECOMMENDATION # 13

## Be aware of intra-racial/ethnic tensions that might exist among students.

The United States is a nation of immigrants. History shows that tensions between the different races and ethnic groups have always existed. We must become aware of and be alert for serious strains that may also exist among students from the same race or ethnic groups, that is, intra-race/ethnic tensions. For example, Hispanic students who are born and raised in the United States might avoid relating with the newly arrived. Hispanic students who are born in the United States are American citizens, prefer to communicate in English, and enroll in regular curricular programs. Conversely, the newly-arrived Hispanics might not have American citizenship, prefer to communicate in Spanish, and enroll in ESL/Bilingual programs.

Likewise, African American students will often look down upon or tease other African American students because their hair may be course, short or kinky. Tension can arise between these students and those who have long, straight or wavy hair. The underlying premise of this tension regarding hair quality is a distorted, culturally-bound notion that having long, straight or wavy hair is having good hair, which is perceived by some African Americans as more "White-like" and therefore, more acceptable and valued as a positive attribute.

# RECOMMENDATION # 14

## Be aware of the African American and Hispanic students' need to "code-switch."

Many African American and Hispanic students are likely to live in two different cultures- the American mainstream and their own. The language, values, beliefs, etc. of the students' home culture might be different from that of their school culture. They live in two different worlds. These students might have the need to "code switch," that is, change their language or outward behavioral manifestations to successfully navigate each cultural challenge they encounter. For example, some Hispanic students might switch from English to Spanish to insulate themselves from perceived threats. African Americans might change from Standard English to Ebonics to avoid being perceived by their same-race peers as "acting White."

# RECOMMENDATION # 15

**Be aware of African American and Hispanic students' resistance to seeking help from staff members they perceive as different from themselves.**

Teachers, guidance counselors, social workers and other support staff members must be aware that some African American and Hispanic students resist seeking help because they think that the staff will not understand or might not care about issues related to their race or ethnicity, immigration status, financial status, level of language acquisition, isolation, etc. School staff members who have direct contact with African American and Hispanic students should enroll in professional development opportunities that provide greater understanding and sensitivity regarding these issues. These staff members must also learn and exhibit verbal and non-verbal behaviors that provide the comfort level and confidence these students need when reaching out for help.

# RECOMMENDATION # 16

## Apply the following "To Do" list when mentoring or counseling African American and Hispanic students.

When mentoring or counseling African American and Hispanic students, I must:

1. Promote, before anything else, an authentic rapport.
2. Create an environment in which students perceive me as a person who truly cares.
3. Recognize the uniqueness of the individual student to resist stereotyping.
4. Avoid becoming defensive or de-legitimizing the students' problems.
5. Provide students with the coping skills needed to resist self-pity, externalizing blame and/or internalizing negative messages that may reflect societal biases.
6. Provide students with the strategies needed to maneuver successfully between inter- and intra-race/ethnic peer groups.

# RECOMMENDATION # 17

## Implement programs that proactively address anti-social behaviors.

Research shows that African American and Hispanic students are over represented in disciplinary actions (detentions, suspensions and expulsions) resulting from inappropriate behaviors in school.

We recommend that schools, at all levels, provide students with opportunities to learn about the negative personal and community impact of antisocial behaviors such as bullying, gang-affiliation, drug or alcohol abuse, etc. These opportunities can be provided through student focus groups, student conferences or special school-wide campaigns.

# RECOMMENDATION # 18

## Make existing teen-pregnancy prevention programs culturally relevant.

According to the *National Vital Statistics Reports* 2010, African American and Hispanic youth comprised nearly 60% of U.S. teen births in 2009, although they represented only 35% of the total population of 15–19 year old females. Many high schools provide educational programs to prevent teen-pregnancy. We are recommending that school administrators and staff members operating these programs evaluate the curricular content to ensure that it is culturally relevant to the girls.

A girl's culture will determine the way she perceives a pregnancy. A curricular program that only addresses the negative consequences of getting pregnant at an early age is not sufficient. For example, a 15-year old girl is a minor in the American mainstream culture, but considered a full grown woman in other cultures. African American and Hispanic girls might see having a baby as a life experience that brings some sort of fulfillment. Undocumented

Hispanic girls may view having a baby that is born in the United States as leverage for staying in the country.

It is for these reasons that we recommend teen pregnancy prevention programs to infuse in their curriculums alternative options for girls to self-actualize and improve the quality of their lives. We recommend that the person(s) assigned to facilitate the program have a deep understanding of the cultural nuances regarding pregnancy.

# RECOMMENDATION # 19

**Increase Hispanic student exposure to role models.**

African American students are often exposed to other African Americans who have experienced academic and life successes through special school events. As a result of this exposure, the "yes, I can!" mantra can have a real meaning. On the other hand, Hispanic students are mostly exposed to other Hispanics who have not experienced successful careers and public acclaim. Because we refer to African Americans and Hispanics as minorities, there is a tendency to assume a sameness of these groups and expect that a successful African American will suffice as a suitable role model for Hispanic students. We highly recommend that, when planning special student events, school administrators make an extra effort to include Hispanic presenters.

# RECOMMENDATION # 20

**Learn more about the negative impact that being undocumented has upon students' personal lives and the schools' AYP reports.**

Undocumented Hispanic high school students find themselves facing a wide range of challenges. They need to be mobile, but are unable hold a driver's license. They need to work to support themselves and their families, but cannot legally hold part-time jobs. They want to pursue a post-secondary education, but do not qualify for financial aid. "They are dammed if they do, and dammed if they don't."

It is for these reasons that we recommend that staff members who work in schools with large Hispanic populations be more informed about the challenges that undocumented students and their families face. In addition, they need to provide undocumented students strategies that can help them pursue academic success despite the inherent difficulties. These strategies may include:

1. Keeping an open mind regarding educational prospects, financial aid, and work opportunities outside of the United States – including in their country of origin.

2. Acquiring knowledge and skills for searching financial aid sources that do not require a social security number - both in and out of the United States.

3. Attaining coping skills for dealing with the anxiety and fear caused by their undocumented status such as positive self-talk, meditation, relaxation techniques, faith-based beliefs, etc.

4. Participating in support groups made up of students who are facing the same challenges.

Students who are undocumented do not have the impetus to achieve academic success or do well on the PSAE. Therefore, we further recommend that school stakeholders inform the community at large about the intrinsic problems that exist when schools are held accountable for the academic achievement of undocumented students.

# RECOMMENDATION # 21

## Celebrate the contributions of African Americans and Hispanics to the development of our nation.

In many ways, our nation is divided and a divided nation cannot prevail. In response to this fact we must do whatever it takes to promote national unity. People are more likely to unite when there is a sense of belonging. Therefore, we recommend that elementary, middle and high schools sponsor classroom activities and school-wide events that promote greater understanding of the African American and Hispanic cultures. These programs should recognize and celebrate the contributions that these two ethnic groups have made to the development of our nation.

When planning these initiatives, we must avoid the tendency to solely emphasize accomplishments in the arts and sports arenas. It is imperative that all students learn about the significant historical roles that these two ethnic groups have played in the military, political, economic, and scientific arenas.

These initiatives, both at the classroom or school-wide levels, have proven to build self-esteem, self-confidence and most of all, a sense of belonging or inclusion. They also motivate minority students to continue the legacy of making this nation a better place for all.

# RECOMMENDATION # 22

**Modify the school's esthetic appearance to promote appreciation for cultural differences.**

The school building esthetics, that is, the pictures, bulletin boards, posters, art displays, etc. provide subliminal messages to any observer. In many cases, African American and Hispanic do not find any positive references to their race or ethnic heritage in their school buildings. A student receives the unintended subliminal message that "I am invisible." We recommend that school administrators pay close attention to the messages that may unintentionally be communicated within their schools' physical environments. When considering school esthetics, we must ensure that African American and Hispanic students' heritage and accomplishments are included in the displays throughout the school building.

# RECOMMENDATION # 23

**Plan, design and implement curricular programs that address African American and Hispanic historical and contemporary trends and issues.**

In the state of Illinois, 40% of the student population belongs to the African American and Hispanic racial/ethnic groups. It is predicted that what we call minorities today will become the majority in the future. In spite of this, most students graduate from high school having little knowledge regarding African Americans and/or Hispanics.

We advise that school districts plan, design and implement courses that address African American and Hispanic histories and contemporary issues. Courses like this can not only validate students who feel marginalized, but also promote understanding and unity across the entire student body. They will also help all students be better prepared to function in our multicultural society.

# RECOMMENDATION # 24

**Increase school districts' efforts to attract, recruit and retain African American and Hispanic administrators and staff members.**

When school administrators and staff members survey the demographic landscape of students in their schools, they observe a kaleidoscope of colors. Conversely, when students view the school staffs' demographic landscape, they do not see a representation of themselves. This perceived lack of equitable representation may lead to students' perceptions that the administration is reluctant to hire staff members of color or that there are no qualified African American or Hispanic candidates.

We highly recommend that school districts' administrations plan and implement initiatives to attract, recruit and retain African American and Hispanic administrators and staff members. All students benefit from this diversity as minority staff members are more likely to expose students to diverse cultures and world-wide perspectives on living, learning, and leadership. These staff members can also build and improve upon student-staff relationships that can lead to better academic and behavioral outcomes.

.

# RECOMMENDATION # 25

## Implement Student Focus/Support Group programs.

Many African American and Hispanic students face challenges that are unique to their life situations. When they attend schools in which they find themselves in the minority, they often feel isolated and uncomfortable. These feelings may fuel the necessity to converse with other same-race/ethnic students using ethnic-unique language or communication patterns to process their individual and collective experiences.

We recommend that schools carefully select a staff person who has the comfort level and grasps the behavioral idiosyncrasies associated with African American and Hispanic students' cultures. This staff member should facilitate structured student focus groups during or right after school hours. These focus groups can afford valuable insights regarding students' thoughts and feelings about subjects of interest and provide students with strategies to face their challenges.

# RECOMMENDATION # 26

## Utilize collateral support for improving the academic achievement of African American and Hispanic students.

It has been said, "It takes a village to raise a child." Schools cannot and should not carry the sole responsibility of closing the academic achievement gaps that exist between African American and Hispanic students and their White and Asian peers.

We recommend that schools and/or districts make use of available collaborative support such as civic, community and faith-based organizations, volunteer organizations, etc. to assist in improving the academic and behavioral performances of students of color. These organizations not only have the vision, passion and the human capital, but can also provide role models or mentors who have a vested interest in increasing the academic achievement of African American and Hispanic students.

# RECOMMENDATION # 27

**Create a District-level function responsible for overseeing the schools' efforts to minimize the achievement gaps.**

Educational leaders know that what is monitored usually gets done. Good intentions alone are not sufficient to create change. Proven-to-work recommendations may sound beneficial, they will not be effective unless consistently executed and closely monitored. We recommend that the district or school administration assign staff members to analyze each recommendation to determine which are most appropriate for increasing the academic achievement of their schools' minority students. After choosing , the staff members must:

1. Determine the steps required for effective implementation.

2. Describe the process that will be used to monitor the execution of the programs.

3. Assess the effectiveness of the recommendation(s).

4. Create a report for review by all school stakeholders. .

# FINAL THOUGHTS

# FINAL THOUGHTS

## A Call for Action

It is our sincere hope that upon completing *Voices*, you will seriously reflect upon the following questions:

1. What is your view of the African American and Hispanic students' opinions regarding their same-race/ethnic peers' lack of academic achievement?
2. What do you believe to be the reasons for the achievement disparity that exists between these two ethnic groups and their White and Asian peers?
3. How does that disparity make you feel?
4. What actions can you take in response to the DuPage County ROE's recommendations for closing the achievement gaps?

Each year, another group of African American and Hispanic students embarks upon their educational journey. What will be in store for them when they reach 12th grade? We sincerely hope that they will surpass the minimal success level of all too many of their predecessors.

Upon answering the questions above and any others that you may have, we implore you to respond to the moral imperative of closing our nation's decades-long academic achievement gaps. By doing so, you have a personal opportunity to be part of the solution to this critical educational challenge.

If we keep doing the same thing and expecting different results, we all know how that ends. What options remain? Please consider adopting the recommendations presented in this book that are appropriate for your school. While implementing any intervention is not a simple feat, it is critical if our nation is to reclaim its educational prominence in the world and ensure that all students have an equitable chance to succeed in America.

In Dr. Ruscitti's words, "We can do it! We have the expertise, the political will and the goodness of heart! After all, isn't that what Americans do when faced with a moral imperative?"

# ACKNOWLEDGEMENTS

# ACKNOWLEDGEMENTS

We want to recognize the following people for the role they played in making the writing of this book possible:

## DuPage County Board Members

*Our deepest debt of gratitude is given to the DuPage County Board members who had the foresight and dedication to education to support the Building Bridges of Understanding initiative which eventually led to the publication of this book. The board members saw the need to study the achievement gaps and develop programming to ensure the success of all students. They are truly committed to education and the students of DuPage County. This investment in our schools, students and communities will pay dividends well into the future.*

## DuPage County's African American and Hispanic Students

*Our African American and Hispanic students trusted us, poured out their hearts and articulated both verbally and in writing their feelings and thoughts regarding the academic achievement gaps that exist between them and their White and Asian peers. What we learned from these students amplified our vision and moved us to find innovative ways to increase the academic achievement of all students.*

## DuPage County's School Administrators, Teachers and Support Staff

*Our county's school administrators, teachers and support staff made possible the hundreds of group and individual student interviews that were conducted in the county's high schools during the past six years. Their desire to learn from the students and determination to help them reach higher levels of academic success has been a source of inspiration.*

## DuPage County's Regional Superintendent of Schools, Dr. Darlene Ruscitti

*Our Regional Superintendent of Schools Dr. Darlene Ruscitti shared the vision and provided the leadership needed to explore the African American and Hispanic students' perspectives regarding academic achievement gaps. She was the force behind the publication of this book, providing the impetus to share both what we have learned and concrete strategies that can help these two ethnic groups improve their academic performance.*

# ABOUT THE AUTHORS

# ABOUT THE AUTHORS

Dr. Lourdes Ferrer and Mr. Stephen Garlington both work as education consultants for the Regional Office of Education (ROE) of DuPage County, in the state of Illinois. Lourdes and Stephen bring to the table two diverse perspectives regarding the academic achievement gaps. As a team of writers, they offer more than 60 years of combined professional experience helping more African American and Hispanic students improve the quality of their lives through a quality education.

## Lourdes

Growing up in a disadvantaged family in Puerto Rico, Lourdes soon learned that education was the way out of the poverty cycle. This understanding led her to complete a Bachelor's Degree in Mathematics at the University of Puerto Rico in Puerto Rico and begin teaching mathematics at the school secondary level. She  left Puerto Rico in 1979 to do community development work in

Guatemala. Her work consisted of establishing and directing schools, an orphanage, feeding centers, clinics and launching health campaigns across the country. With the assistance from Guatemalan government officials Lourdes procured resources from international non-profit organizations. Her experience in community development was the catalyst that led her to choose Research, Evaluation, and Measurement as the focus of her Master's Degree at the University del Valle in Guatemala.

When she immigrated to the United States in 1990, she had to overcome enormous financial, linguistic, and cultural barriers to pursue the American Dream. She became a secondary school mathematics teacher in Dade and Palm Beach counties. She went on to complete her Doctor's Degree in Leadership at Florida Atlantic University in Florida and took a position as a School Improvement and Assessment Specialist for the School District of Palm Beach County. Her responsibilities included leading No Child left behind (NCLB) staff development opportunities for teachers and school administrators, as well as speaking at community forums regarding the same issues.

She joined the DuPage ROE team of consultants on June of 2006. For the past six years she has been assisting school districts in DuPage County and other districts across the nation to create data streams through research, developing curricular programs for Hispanic parents including *Navigating the American Educational System* and *Sit in the Driver's Seat*. She has trained teachers, school administrators and communities at large, to help more African American and Hispanic students achieve greater academic success. She is also the author of

*Hispanic Parental Involvement - Ten Competencies Schools Need to Teach Hispanic Parents* and another for Hispanic parents: *Sientese en la Silla del Conductor* (Sit in the Driver's Seat).

## Stephen

Growing up in an economically disadvantage home environment, Stephen's family moved from New York City to the suburbs of

Westchester County to afford him better opportunities to thrive and attain the benefits of a good education. Stephen's early experiences with poverty, education and strong parental guidance, laid the foundation for his passion in helping others to meet their academic potential. Stephen spent a significant amount of years directing "at risk" youth education and training programs across the country. In addition, he has also provided social and clinical services in educational environments. His involvement in this kind of work and desire to improve his services propelled him to complete his Bachelor's Degree in Human Services at the Sojourner Douglass College in Baltimore, Maryland. After achieving this success, he immediately enrolled at the University of Maryland in Baltimore and attained his Master's Degree in Clinical Social Work and later his state clinical license. After reaching these academic milestones, Stephen continued servicing the youth of this country through educational positions with the government at state, regional and federal levels. Mr. Garlington joined the DuPage ROE team of consultants on September 2007 to continue his fulfillment for working with students, parents, community, and other stakeholders toward closing the academic achievement gaps.

# VOICES

# VOICES